1967 · PRESSCRAFT PAPERS · BENZONIA MICHIGAN

Wing-borne

- - - - - - by Gwen Frostic

In sudden flight the birds go by
ascending into the boundless sky - - - -
bumblebees hum in the open fields
on delicate fairy wings - - -

- - - and seeds have wings
and dragonflies - - - -
and tiny spotted ladybugs . . . .

Wing-borne - - - - - - -
these things are ever free
to rise from the earth
and sail with the winds . . . . .

Wing-borne - - - - - - - -
we - too - can rise to the heights
where clouds recede
in the clear blue sky - - - - - -
we can reach far up and touch the stars - -
and feel the passionate joy of being . . . . .

- - - - - - - the wings of the mind
are strong and free . . . .

All the wild things sing their songs
     from the hilltops - -
          from the marshlands - - -

     there is sunshine
          there are shadows
               songs of rain among the trees - - -

     of the mysteries
          of the beauty
               of the faith in miracles

each one sings a separate song
          blending into one great hymn

     the symphony of life eternal . . . .

- - - - little plants rise from the earth each spring

birds sing in loveliness - - - - - -

frogs trill into the night
          as the stars come into view - - -

moss grows on an old old log
          bright and fresh and green - - - -

- - - - these things do not live for me - - - - - - - - -

- - - - - - - - - - but because they are - - -

- - - - - - I am . . . .

Diversity - - - - - -

      even in the grasses . . . . . .

Although following an inherent
pattern - each blade of grass takes
the air - the water - - - and the
energy of the sun and develops an
individualistic life - - - - - - - in
freedom and beauty . . . .

Diversity - - - - -

      and loveliness - - - - -

out in the open fields - - - under
the sunlit sky . . . .

To those whose quest is beauty - -

- - - - - - - - - beauty is universal

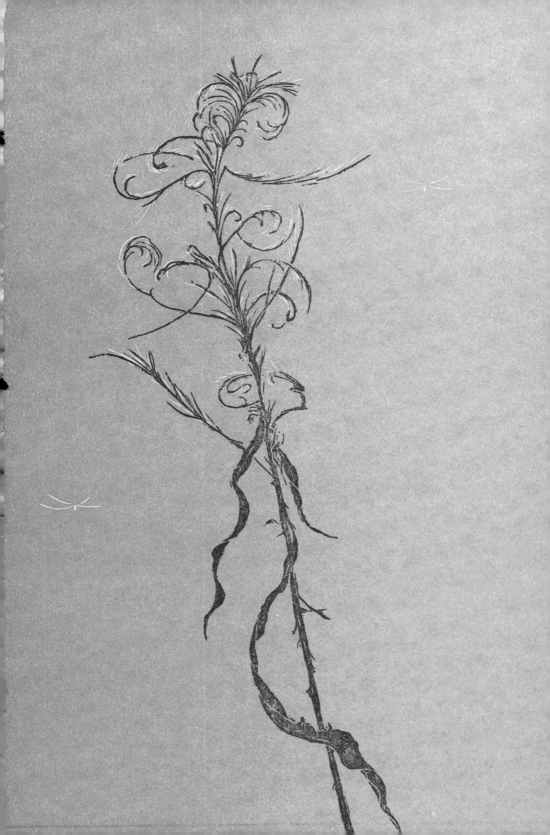

There are fanciful little figures
            in the driftwood on the beach

    dried grasses sway and wave their leaves
            dancing to the rhythm of the winds

    There are faces on the burls of trees
            whimsical forms in stones
                        and clouds

        and

cedars stand like ghosts
risen from the earth
after the snow has fallen

secret springs of enchantment flow
when imagination frees the soul

- - - - - - - the bee is merely gathering food

Each life lives unto itself - - - -
　　　　　- - - yet serves eternity . . . . .

Without the millions of fluttering wings
　　　　　the world of flowers would not exist - -

without the world of flowers and plants
　　　　　the things with wings could have no life - - -

- - - - - - - the bee is merely gathering food
　　　　　- - the flowers maturing into seed - -
　　　- - each intent on its own pursuit . . . .

Upon all lives each life depends - - - -
　　　　　- - - - - the lives of flowers and birds - - -
　　　　　　　　of trees - - - and man - - -
　　the very earth from which life grows
　　　　　　　is recreated by that life . . . .

Each shall develop unto itself
　　　　　and from within must ever grow - - -
　　for when a thing shall cease to grow
　　　　　it ceases　then　- to be a life - - -
　　　　　it grows to live - - - -
　　　　　　it lives to grow - - - -

　　　- - - - - an independent life - -
and yet - - - - interdependent upon all life . . . .

- - - each intent on its own pursuit . . . .

A little seed drops to an old gnarled stump - - -
- - - - - a shoot starts up - - - -
- - - and a tree will grow - - -
nourished by the stump that is
returning to earth . . . .

Its roots will soon encircle the stump
and reach far down to the soil below - - -
as the stump is slowly becoming fertile ground
where new life will flourish
in aeons to come . . . .

By the time the stump has completed its cycle - - -
the tree will stand strong and firm - - - - -
- - it will brace itself against the storms
and from the earth
will draw its life . . . .

The great impelling force to grow
is intense and supreme
in the world of plants - - - - -

- - - - - even in a seed
that never reached earth . . . .

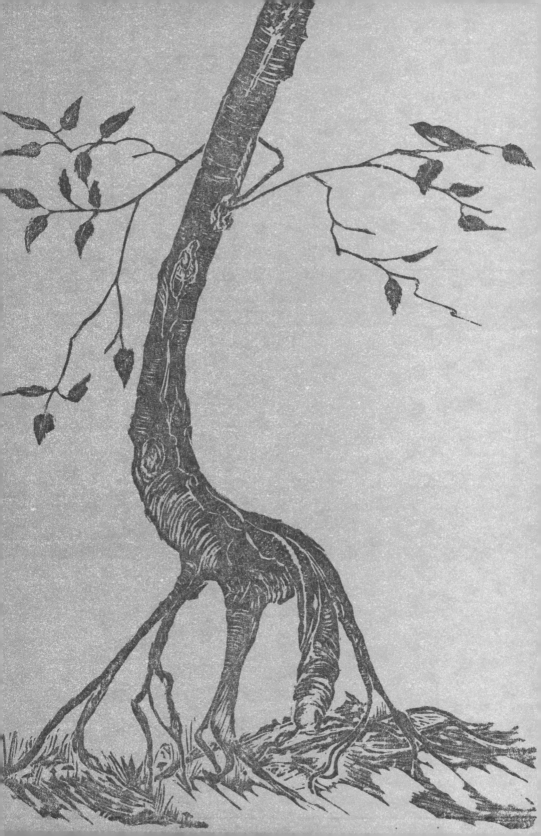

A leaf quivers at the end of a branch - - - -
- - - - - - a blade of grass sways gently
the force that moves that tiny leaf
- - - and makes the grass bend low
is the one that tosses the waters high - - - - -
and roars through the tops of trees
in sudden bursts of wildness . . . . .

It brings soft rains to the waking year - - -
and scatters seeds when their wings
have grown . . . .
Snow or sand - - - - - -
earth or rock - - -
it moves and shapes them all - - - - - - -
determines how a tree shall grow
and where the birds shall fly . . . . .
It's wild and free - - - - - - - -
gentle - - - - and subdued - - - - - -
- - - - only the wind - - - - -
just air in motion - - -
- - - - a simple thing - -
- - - - - - - - the wind . . . .

A quiet pond embodying the stirring beauty - - -
the serenity - - the intense activity of life . . .

Suddenly concentric circles widen upon the
water - - - - a fish leaps into the air and back
into the cool pool . . . . The pond is a smooth
mirror again - - - - - - as a beaver breaks the
spell - - - - leaving a widening V of ripples in
his wake . . . .

Frogs are calling in many tempos - - dragonflies
in glistening colors fly close to the water . . . . .
Each tree - bush - - and stump - - - - - - each
reed and blade of grass is individually and

collectively reflected by the still water - - - - -
doubling the magnificence of spring . . . .
A great blue heron flies over - - - - - the little
green heron stands on a fallen tree - - - - - his
neck stretched high - - - - his crest extended
- - - - - and they - - too - - are doubled . . . . .
Water-striders are sliding over the surface of the
pond - - - making dimples in it - - - but not
breaking it . . . . A catkin falls from a
willow tree - - - - and the ripples begin anew
- - - - with each breath of wind the reflections
become a mass of wavery hues . . . .
The swamp sparrow is singing - - - - - - and the
warblers are coming in . . . .

Each thing has a wondrous life to live - - - - - in varying spans of time - - - - - trees have many years to grow - - - - insects have but hours - - - - - - - - trees will fall - - - and insects die as time creates new life and blends it with the old - - - - perpetuating the unbroken rhythm of the universe . . . .

As long as there are trees - - - - - - - there will be insects among the leaves and in the crevices of the bark - - - - - - as long as insects grow and reproduce their own - - - - - - the warblers will come back . . . . And little ponds will always be a source of life and beauty . . . .

Only with the rain - - -

    do the colors of the rainbow span the sky - - -
    the buds of the maples are brighter - - - - .
    old rocks in the fields glisten - - - - -
    the spider's web becomes a fragile jewel

All life takes on more beauty - - - - - -
    when there is rain . . . .

Alone she sits - - - -

    through rains and storms - - - -

        instinctively faithful to her trust . . . . .

Long hours become long days - - - and on through the cycle of the silver moon - - - - but time is not when one has found a mission to fulfill . . . .

Tall grasses grow around her - - - - - and golden dandelions turn to white - - - - - then comes a day when the shells crack open - - - - - - - little heads appear - - - - - - and downy ducks emerge . . . . . .

They feel the warmth of the shining sun - - - - - - - - they know their mother's call - - - - - - - - to the pond she takes her brood and shows them what is food . . . .

They dart about - - - they dive and swim with all the zest of youth . . . . Carefully she watches them - - - - yet - - - lets them know the freedom that growing things must have . . . .

Buttercups and daisies bloom - - - Queen Ann's lace and cattails - - - each - has its hour of glory - - - while the little ducks are growing - - - - - - feathers replace their down - - - - and they begin to have the markings of the ones that gave them birth . . . .

Another spring — — some of these ducks will wait the long hours through - - - and other little ducks will swim and dive - - - - - - just as they do now . . . .

Out in the woods among tall trees
    where flowers blossom and birds build nests
- - - - - there are no contradictions . . . .

From the simplest lichen on a tree - - - -
        to the most complex life that lives - - -
    the act of growth transcends all else . . . . . .

A snail is born close to the earth - - - - -
        it lives and grows upon the land - - - -
        it eats to grow - -
                sometime - - - in turn
        it will be eaten - - - -
            that something else may live - - - - -
    there is no waste of time - - - or lives
        each death sustains another life . . . .

The wind that roars and uproots trees - - - - -
        is clearing space for other growth - - - - -
    that wind will also carry seeds - - - - - - -
        and plants will rise along its path . . . .

The millions of seeds from a single plant - - - -
all serve to continue life on earth - - - -
some will grow to be great trees
others become food for birds and mice - - - -

each a very minute part - - - -
of a great majestic harmony . . . . .

The alertness of the birds - - -
the intensity of the plants to grow - - - -
the constant watchfulness of each - - - - -
to protect its right to be
- - - and to become . . . .

This is life - - - - in all its forms - -
so simple
so wondrous
so everlasting . . . .

There is no time for inconsistency - - -
eternal life is being served . . . .

he insatiable curiosity

the vitality

the eagerness

of youth - - - - -

Only man

can keep it - - - -

- - - - - - and

only if he will . . . . . .

The source of all the energy of earth

a revolving mass of light . . . .

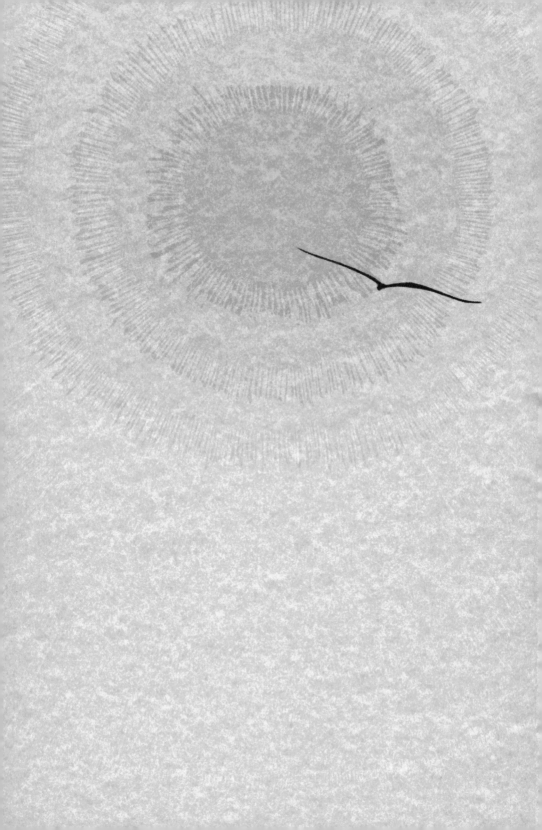

Around it in a measured pace the spinning world is traveling - - - - creating night and day - - - the months and the years - - - - - - summer - - - - winter - - - - - spring and fall . . . .

Into the air that surrounds the earth - - - - - clouds are forming - - - - - - clouds of wondrous splendor - - - - - - dense vapors - - - and tiny wisps of crystaled air - - - - - - expansive - - ascending mists - - - catching the rays of the sun and bouncing them back and forth until the cloud itself is light . . . .

Clouds that are heavy with rain - - - - - and storm clouds through which the rays cannot pass for days - - - - - - - yet - - - above and beyond - - - - the sun is shining . . . .

From the soil of the earth the sun brings
forth life - - - - seeds sprout - - - and tiny plants
rise to reach the light . . . .

The countless leaves upon each tree - - - the
leaves of every flower - - - - - - each blade of grass
sometime - - - somehow will turn that the sun will
shine upon it - - - and - thereby make the one
connecting link between the sun and all the life on
earth . . . .

When the day is ending grasses of the dunes
cast long shadows across the sands - - - - and the
sun reaches only the tops of the trees . . . .

- - - - - - long red rays - - - - -
- - - - moving clouds - - - -
the huge sun on our horizon - - - -
a great panorama of color - - - - -
and another day is done . . . .

Tall trees are silhouetted in the twilight
- - - - the evening thrush is singing . . . . . .

- now - - - - the light of the sun
is reflected by the moon - - - - -
the night is filled with loveliness - - - - - -
the soul of man with awe . . . .

It stands apart - - - - -

and yet it is

a part of all the living earth . . . . . .

The lines of the wind blown sand on the dunes

- - - of the snow as it falls in beautiful drifts

the lines of the clouds

in the sky above - - - - -

and the water that washes upon the sands - - -

forever and ever these lines repeat - - - - - -

always and always

each one is unique . . . .

Dry leaves rise in a gust - - - -

- - - tiny birds in little flocks - - -

gulls soar - - - - -

insects swarm - - - -

seeds whirl and sail - - -

millions of times the formation repeats - - - -

each time - - - - each thing

unto itself is unique . . . .

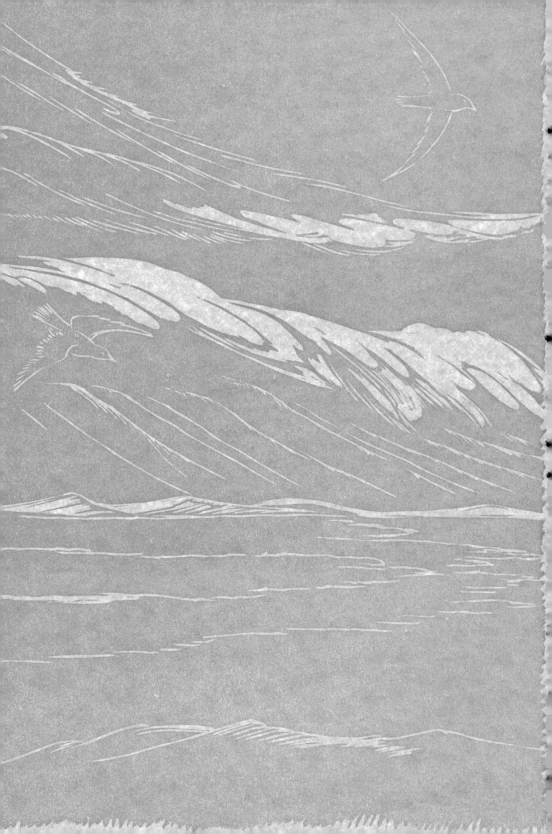

A tree reaches up toward the sky - - - - -
        with graceful limbs and intricate twigs
        - - - or - with branches that are
            massive - knotty - - - and gnarled -
in the pattern of the trees that bore its seed . . . . .
    Aeons shall pass - - -
            as the pattern repeats - - - -

        this day - - - - - -
            this tree - - - - - - - -
                is a tree unique . . .   .

All the stars on a clear still night - - - - -
        all the leaves of a single tree - - - - - -
            the many ideas that one may have - - - -
over and over
            the basic concept repeats - - - - -

    yet - - - - -
        each star - - - -
            each leaf - - - - -
            and idea - - - - -
                is unique . . . .